Self-Lover's Only Guidebook

Excerpts from TeamCWCM
Transformation & Change Guide
Practices for Self-Paced Study

© 2026 All Rights Reserved
ISBN: 9798244399912

Cacique Operating Artist Santos S.O.U.L.
"I'm Changing My World, By Changing Me"
@teamcwcm
www.teamcwcm.com

This workbook includes excerpts from the TeamCWCM Transformation and Change Guide©
TeamCWCM is a Methodology & philanthropic Network of GlocalSOUL Edutainment.
All our programs start with and center Self-Love.

This is (1) of (5) comprehensive Guidebooks & Courses.
(ME, DREAM, TEAM, WE, CHANGE)

Our Overall Program outcomes are intended to Inspire, Entertain, Educate, & Empower Healthy sustainable Collective Change centering Individual Self Transformation.

To learn more about the Methodology, receive 1 on1 or small group coaching from an authorized TeamCWCM facilitator, access the virtual library and Full Course, please visit www.teamcwcm.com or email team@teamcwcm.com

This Guidebook is dedicated to my ancestors returned, my children; I love you, thank you for your patience, love, and empathy, to their peers, all the children of their generation, those yet to come, and the healing of each of our inner Children! This book is also dedicated to my Teachers, Family, and the billions of people committed to creating healthy sustainable Change & Transformation in their lives, aligned with the greater good of our planet. We see you! Together we got this!

TeamCWCM is a network of people, places, resources, and ideas rooted in local communities worldwide of all frequencies and walks of life, committed to consistently exploring ways of refining systems of self-transformation and healthy sustainable collective change and liberation aligned with nature.

I have been honored to share excerpts from this Curriculum Guide in Elementary, Middle, and High Schools, Colleges, Universities, Corporate Learning Communities, Professional Development trainings, shared as Home School Curriculum, in 1 on 1 coaching sessions, Community Groups and with friends and loved ones. Many of these practices and concepts have served me deeply on my own journey of Transformation, accepting & navigating Change.

Thank you for receiving the vision. May it heal & prosper all areas of your life!

"I'm Changing My World, by Changing Me"

Santos "Glocal" S.O.U.L.

Cacique & Founder

GlocalSoul Edutainment

Self-Lover's Only Guidebook

Table of Contents

About the Author & Method	pg i, iii
TeamCWCM Overview	pg 3
Getting Started	pg 4
"I Love My"… List	pg 5
"Relation-Ship"	pg 12
InnerG	pg 14
Word, Sound, Power!	pg 21
Affirmations of Change	pg 22
Self-Love Standard	pg 24
Element of Change	pg 34
I Respect Myself	pg 39
Seed of Transformation	pg 50
Ancestors	pg 53
T.E.A.M. Work	pg 58
Self-Love Agreement	pg 63
Seasons of Change	pg 66
About TeamCWCM	pg 70
Glossary & Fundamental Concepts	pg 71
Self-Love Routine Charts	pg 72-85
Life Work (For Print)	pg 86

Self-Lover's Only Guidebook

I LOVE MYSELF

It all begins with SELF-LOVE!

Peace Power and Love to YOU, Beautiful, Powerful, Being! Thank you so much for your time, presence, and **InnerG** on this journey! Your participation and investment in yourself and this Work with TeamCWCM, is my D.R.E.A.M. coming to bloom! Hopefully it will activate a part of yours too! I'll do my best to briefly explain. Most know me as "Santos". I AM A life LOVER. I spend a lot of time in my heart space. While it may be one of the most PowerFULL places to express from, the heart center is not always the securest place to live in, unregulated and unaware, given the current state of the World we collectively share. (The heart center is great for visioning a beautiful harmonious new way of thriving on the planet, and for writing love songs!)

I'm also a **"Sifu"** or teacher and steward of various Healing Modalities and Martial Sciences for over 20 years. I am also the youngest and final formal student of my first teacher. Until I pass them on, I strive to take best care in stewarding these potent practices and exercise discernment in how they are shared. These practices of InnerG Cultivation are deeply important to me. They found me in my late teens, amidst a huge personal growth period after just moving to the southern U.S. from my small community in Japan. It was at this time I met my first teacher & Root Guru; he shared that I could truly change my life, my world, and even possibly subtly influence my DNA. Very young, and not quite mature enough to comprehend his suggestion, or the potency of some very advanced healing arts and monastic practices, I threw myself all in, very ambitious to Change "my" World and to Change "the" World around me!

The Self-Lover's Journey, and other offerings from the TeamCWCM Methodology came from this inspiration. Included in the next few pages are some introductory mindfulness and breathwork practices to support you along your Self-Love Journey, alone and or with loved ones. To learn more, access videos, classes and workshops centering tools of self-regulation and exploration, please visit: www.masterpeacetaichi.com. **This Self-Lover's Only Guide is the foundation and prerequisite to all other TeamCWCM course work.**

Welcome to a whole season of Self-Love!

Are you ready to Activate and Explore a new outlook on life by "Centering Self-Love"?
_____
_____
_____

Are you Centered?
_____
_____
_____

What does "Healthy Selfish" mean to you?
_____
_____
_____

In Changing your World (your unique lifestyle, Worldview, & physical, mental, emotional reality). Let's first start with the "ME" or Self! (Inner Work, Inner Alchemy). We all have duties and commitments outside of ourselves. This is an invitation to return to your center, your core values, goals & routines, then overflow into all other parts of your reality. Embrace, Accept, Explore, Celebrate SELF from a state of Love!

Scan the QR Code or go to SantosSoulMusic.com for Musical Accompaniment to your Journey!

Declare out loud: "I LOVE MYSELF"

Take this Season of Self-Love at a pace that is sustainable for you!

Pace yourself, consistent progress is better than attempting to digest and complete everything at once. This Guide is Comprehensive, each lesson builds upon the next. In this Season of Transformation and Change, we are focused on the intrapersonal relationship to Self or the "ME". Allow 1 week to prepare and at least 1-week Review period. It's always a great time to start. Repeat these activities and affirmations as often as you'd like any time or season. This Guidebook could take you 30 days, 60 days, 90 days, possibly a year or more! We suggest you give your best effort to complete, review, and repeat these activities within a 90+1-day period.

INTRO, OVERVIEW & AGREEMENTS
(1 week minimum to 1.5 month maximum)

Create a personal Self-Love affirmation and sign your Self-Love Agreement. This document is the final page in this GuideBook. **Set aside time in your schedule per instructions.** (You may desire to photocopy or tear out your "Self-Love Agreement" and place it as a visual reminder of your commitment to your Self Love Journey.)

ME (SELF)
(2 weeks minimum to 3 months maximum)
Self-Love & Care, Self-Respect, Self-Centering, Personal Element, and Seed of Self Transformation Ancestors and FAMily Tree.

CLOSING
(1 week review and self-assessment)
Review your self-love journey.
Record a brief video or voice memo documenting your journey.

Please Review what is required to begin thoroughly on the following page.
Thank you for being here! You showed up!

Are you ready to keep your word to yourself, forgive and Love yourself as many times and as long as it takes on this journey?

To begin, you will need:

- Self-Love, Patience, Compassion & will power (for additional support, Inquire about Master Peace Inner Arts)
- A Transformation & Change Journal, specifically focusing on these activities centering Self-Love.
- A minimum of 30 to 90 minutes per day (1/2 of that time in the AM and 1/2 of that time in the evening),
- It is ideal to review visuals you will create, personal affirmations and reflections early upon waking and right before falling asleep.
- A mirror to look into and make eye contact with your own eyes. It's nice if you can get a mirror that only you use, if not, that's fine too.
- One small personal item that symbolizes Radical Self-Love to you.
- Trustworthy companion(s): mentor, exceptional peer, or select FAMily member to consult (recommended but optional)
- Prepare per instructions on the **final page** of this Guidebook entitled "Self Love Agreement" and allow a minimum of 1 hour to Celebrate the beginning of your Journey!
- This is a self-paced Guide. The only competition is with self. In addition to becoming more aware of the rhythms, cycles, and seasons of change within and around you, YOU can take as much time creating the CHANGES YOU desire to experience in YOUR Life. This is only a Guide!

"I Love My...
"A Self-Love List"

1. However, many years you've been alive, list that many attributes or qualities you Love about yourself inside the heart.

2. What parts of you didn't make your list? Write those on the Red area. They are a part of self and deserve love too.

3. List each quality in the form of an "I love my_____" statement. Recite a minimum of 10 at a time Daily in the mirror as part of your Rise or Evening Routine. Can you do this for 30 to 90 days? You can make a personal voice recording to play while waking or exercising. You may like to visibly post these somewhere you see regularly.

Self-Lover's Only Guidebook

What are some Ways that you...?

- Love Yourself
- Respect Yourself
- Trust, Know & Believe in Yourself
- Value Your Unique Individuality
- Experience & enjoy connectedness to others
- Cultivate and Master Your Peace InnerG
- Create and Respond to Changes in Your Reality

What's one specific area of your Life you could Love MORE?

- Mindfulness, Spirituality, Time in Nature
- Wellness, Fitness, Nutrition
- Authentic Expression, Passion, Profession, D.R.E.A.M. Work
- Joy, Play, Rest and Relaxation
- Wealth building & Financial Freedom
- Self-Discipline & Consistent Routines
- Aligned Reciprocal Relationships & Boundaries

Self-Lover's Only Guidebook

What's one way you can achieve this or plan to achieve this?

_____
_____
_____
_____
_____
_____

What is one area in your life you can pour more love into allowing you to overflow into other areas?

_____
_____
_____
_____
_____
_____
_____

Self-Lover's Only Guidebook

What Changes are you willing to make in your life to allow more self-love, self-care, and self-celebration into your daily life?

_____
_____
_____
_____

How often do you Center Yourself each day?

_____
_____
_____
_____

Can you allow 3-5 minutes when you first rise and as you prepare or drift to sleep each night to be "Self-Centered", that is to express gratitude for something you achieved or look forward to achieving. You're doing great at your own pace!

_____
_____
_____
_____

On the outside of this circle write down your favorite self-love activities, and some ways you plan to love yourself more. You may want to redraw this on poster paper and hang it up where you can see it daily or take a photo & add it to the favorites in your phone.

Be Unapologetic about Loving Yourself!

If you are in, or desire to deepen a partnership or relationship with other(s):

This is a deeply personal journey. Do share that you are going deeper into your commitment and practice of Self-Love and Self-Care with those closest to you! You may feel inspired to share insights that come up and some activities within these pages. Please know your journey is your own.

Ask consent to share. Do not impose any of the practices on anyone. Be mindful of your expectations. You will have greater awareness of yourself if you take time with each page. Parts of you may undergo change. Not everyone in your life will be able to grow with you. That's ok. Trust the process and know that by deepening your Self-Love to a point of overflow, all that you love will benefit!

Self-Lover's Only Guidebook

Our Greatest Relation - "Ship" is with Self

All other Relation"Ships" are experienced through the SELF

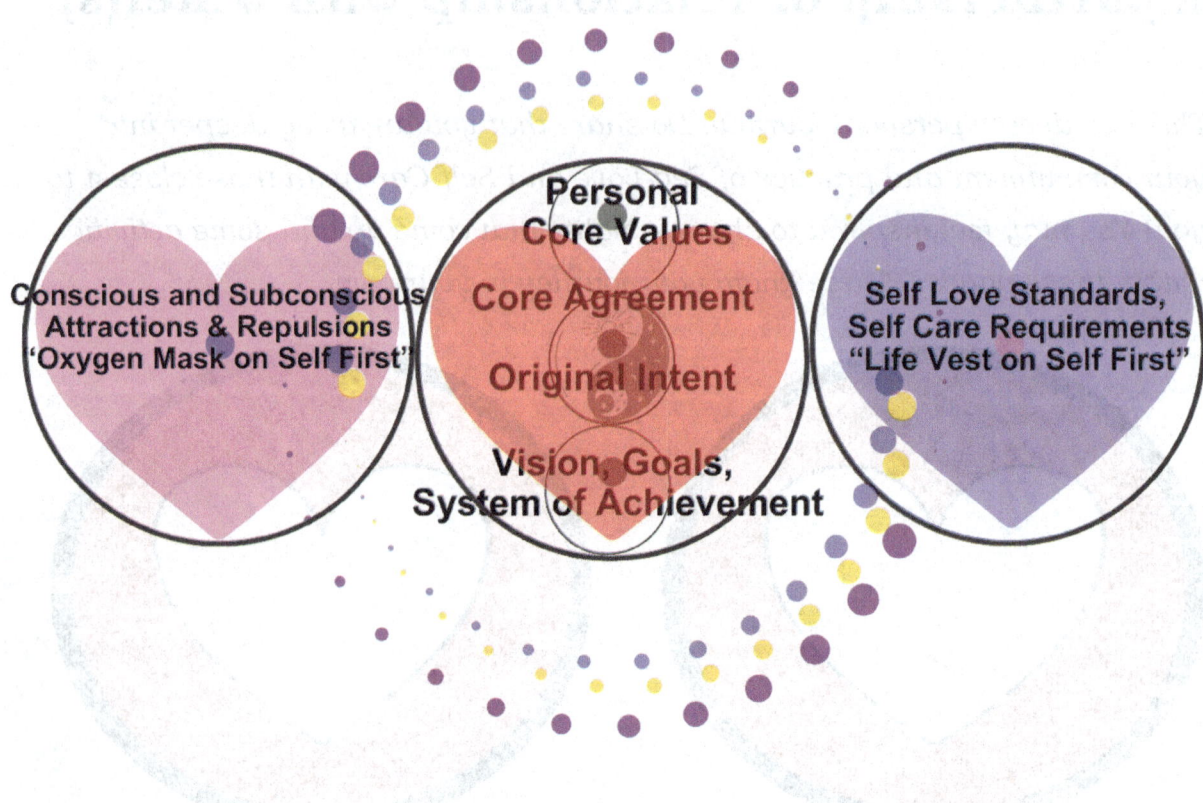

When Navigating the Seas of Life, it's important to know aspects of your own "SHIP", such as your: Agreement with Self, Personal Values, Life Purpose, Aligned Intentions, D.R.E.A.M. lifestyle Vision, Current Mission, Goals, tasks, Daily Routines, Intuitive Decisions.

When we are in full harmonious alignment with ourselves, we can serve our purpose and all our relation"Ships" with life from the "overflow".

In completing and reviewing this GuideBook, we hope you continue to be informed & inspired by more tools & concepts as it relates to your Relation "Ship" with yourself.

Routines, Goals, D.R.E.A.M.

The Journey is...   **...the Destination**

InnerG

IT'S ALL InnerG!

InnerG =

Intention, Focused Presence & Cultivated Internal Energy

Inner Greatness, Inner Guidance, Inner GPS to navigate your Inner Galaxy

Healthy, sustainable Transformation & Change requires effort, clarity, consistency, support and InnerG! Internal Energy is everywhere! It's literally in the air we breathe All existence is vibrating, everything has a Vibe! We already know that Energy is neither created nor destroyed and is in constant motion. The InnerG inside of us, which gives us our vitality, is known in many cultures as: Qi, Prana, Lung, Sekhem, Bio Electricity, Tummo, Siddhi, Ngolo, Ase, and much more. We can learn to harness, cultivate, direct, and refine it. What kind of InnerG do you bring? Your InnerG is a product of your mental, emotional, and physical diet.

G.I.G.O.-Greatness In = Greatness Out, Garbage in = Garbage Out!

We are always Exchanging Energy with people close to us, our environment, nature, and all of life. Our actions, words, and even our thoughts create vibrations and give off energy. Some Actions, Words, and thoughts increase our energy, while others, decrease or drain our energy by affecting our nervous system. Learning to slowly regulate our breathing and cultivate this InnerG is invaluable. Energy changes within the body and in our environment throughout the day, each week, month, and season. It can be further affected by the place we live. Our breath is our greatest regulator of energy within the body. Energy is not InnerG without Intention, focused Attention, and some form of cultivating it, like mindful movement and conscious breathing. What kind of energy do you bring? What people, places, foods, habits and thoughts give you more **SUSTAINABLE** energy? What decreases or drains your Energy?

What Gives you InnerG?

What activities, people, places, ideas, and so on, InnerGize and or drain you?

_____
_____
_____
_____
_____
_____
_____
_____

What kind of energy do you bring?

_____
_____
_____
_____
_____
_____
_____
_____

What people, places, foods, habits and thoughts give you more SUSTAINABLE energy? What decreases or drains your Energy? Draw or write them down.

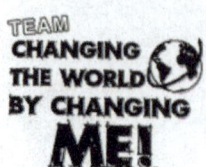

What are some activities, people, places, or ideas that give you PEACE?

_____
_____
_____
_____
_____
_____
_____

Self-Regulation, InnerG Management, and knowing what inspires PEACE, within and around you go a long way on your journey of Transformation & Change.

Self-Lover's Only Guidebook

Clearing Breath

Speaking of InnerG. We'll learn more about Self-Regulation and the Breath as a tool to clear and adjust our InnerG.

Let's learn a mindful movement called "clearing". Take a big inhale in through your nose. Bringing both hands up above your head, palms facing up, slowly reaching as high as they can reach. Imagine you are gathering fresh InnerG above your head.
As you exhale, forming your lips like blowing through a straw, slowly bring your hands down in front of you, palms turning to face the ground, fingers not touching. Follow your hands down with your vision, remember "where your mind goes, InnerG flows".

Imagine you are washing fresh air or InnerG down from above the crown of your head through the soles of your feet. Pushing out all the old air, or stagnant InnerG into the Earth below you.
Do these two more times, inhaling as your hands go up and exhaling fully as your hands go down, in through the nose, out through the mouth, nice and slow each time. This helps settle our nervous system, oxygenates our brain, and gives us a sense of clarity and calm. Do this as often as you need to.

Ok, **We're InnerGized for Change!**

What are some methods and tools you may know that give you clarity and InnerG?

_____
_____
_____
_____
_____
_____
_____
_____
_____

Word-Sound-Power!

We can activate InnerG with how we speak to ourselves and others. Here are some helpful Affirmations.

"I AM a strong Tree Rooted in My Destiny."

"As I heal Myself, I heal others."

"I AM a strong tree rooted in my Ancestry."

"As I heal Myself, I heal my family."

"I AM a Strong tree rooted in healthy, sustainable community."

"As I heal Myself, I heal my World, the planet and all her Kingdoms."

"My health is my wealth."

"Teamwork makes the dream work."

"I'm Changing My World, by Changing Me"

Change is a Constant.

Intentional Change happens moment by moment, breath by breath, one step at a time. You're doing great at your own pace.

AFFIRMATIONS OF CHANGE

START FROM THE BOTTOM AND WORK YOUR WAY UP!

What are some Affirmations you like to use or some that you have heard? We invite you to write them below and if they feel good, recite them in front of a mirror!

_____
_____
_____
_____
_____
_____
_____

Are there any affirmations or encouraging sayings you heard from within your family or community growing up or currently? Write them down. We'll reflect on these later in your journey.

_____
_____
_____
_____
_____
_____
_____

SELF-LOVE STANDARD

HOW DO YOU EXPECT LIFE TO LOVE YOU BACK?

What's your Self-Love Standard?

What is the standard you hold your Self-Love Life to?

_____
_____
_____
_____

This is your "Golden Rule" of Love with All of Life.

What are the ways you confidently expect life to reciprocally meet you?

_____
_____
_____
_____

Take some time to become more mindful and aware of your own latent or clearly expressed desires and expectations.

Do you feel met, felt, heard, and seen by Your SELF?

_____
_____
_____
_____

What is your body saying?

_____
_____
_____
_____

What is your environment or the way you adorn yourself say?

_____
_____
_____
_____

Are you honoring your own personal Self-Love Standard or Golden Rule?

_____
_____
_____
_____

However, we answer these questions, we can <u>know</u>, <u>trust, and believe</u> that **life will match our frequency!**

Practice acknowledging your Self-Love Standard & Authentic relationship with life. Meditate on each of these below: What ways do you delight in loving your life, Self-Loving and Self-Caring for Your SELF?

_____
_____
_____
_____

This can include your InnerGetic/Spiritual, physical, mental, emotional and Cultural hygiene; The Sounds, colors, fabrics, scents, tastes, and sights you enjoy and are naturally attracted to; The pace you prefer and enjoy moving through your day and/or through different experiences.

We can't expect this from others. We can know that how we treat ourselves sets the pitch and tone for how others, and life will treat us. **Complete the circuit with self-first, then overflow!**

What places reflect your standard of self-love? (your bedroom, workspace, transportation, places you visit and socialize in)

_____
_____
_____

What quality of food, drink and nutrition reflect your standard?
___
___
___
___

What people currently in your life reflect your standard of self-love?
___
___
___
___

Does your relationship with wealth, prosperity, stewarding money, currency, and cash flow reflect your Self-Love Standard?
___
___
___
___

Do not compromise your Self-Love standard! Love yourself more! Overflow into all of life around you. Witness the changes. Observe what remains & what naturally fades away. Be open to letting go for greater!

What is your favorite Self-Love Meal?

_____
_____
_____

What foods feel great to your Body?

_____
_____
_____

What foods leave you feeling energized & deeply nourished? Do you have a favorite healthy go to quick snack?

_____
_____
_____

If you have a self-love Meal that you prepare for yourself, schedule some time to prepare it in the coming days. You can even share a photo to your phone. Feel free to share your favorite fruit(s) and veggies with the people you most often share meals with, at home or at work. Your body often calls for what it needs most.

How did you honor each part of you today?

_____
_____
_____
_____
_____
_____
_____

What did you do?

_____
_____
_____
_____
_____
_____
_____
_____

Draw or write out how you honored each part of you today. (For self-love, self-respect. etc.)

Self-Lover's Only Guidebook

Self-Love is the foundation on your journey of Change and Transformation

	S	M	T	W	T	F	S
Self-Love, Self-Care, Esteem Building Routine							
Self-Inquiry, Observation, Mindful Reflection							
Skill and Talent Cultivation & Refinement							
Sharing Gifts, Talents, Skill in your networks reciprocally							
*							
*							

*These categories are TeamCWCM Suggested areas of focus to optimize Sustainable Change and Self Transformation towards your desired results.

Feel free to add specific activities or practices that best serve you.

ELEMENT OF CHANGE

YOU ARE NATURE!

What's your Element?

Metal   Water   Wood   Fire   Earth   Air   Ether or InnerG

If you were to identify with an Element of Nature, what would you choose? You may feel like more than one, however choose one Element as your Dominant Element.
_____
_____

Are you the leader? Life of the party?
_____
_____

Do you keep the balance, seek resolution?
_____
_____

Do you go with the flow? Calm and Mellow?
_____
_____

Always on the go or still and immoveable?
_____
_____

Are you the logical, grounded, practical one?
_____
_____

What's your Element?

Metal   Water   Wood   Fire   Earth   Air   Ether or InnerG

Elements are consistent. They may Change form, as in the way they show up, but they are consistent at authentically staying true to their essence.

Let's Consider Transformation & Change are their own element!

Is there a place in nature where you feel "in your element"?

_____

_____

During this season of Self-Love, visit nature and spend time "in your element" weekly, or as often as inspired to. After choosing an element (you can change your mind or choose a runner up!), what form of your element would you be? (i.e. a flame, a volcano, a soft breeze or a tornado.)

_____

_____

Choosing an element that feels most natural to you and observing how you show up in a group setting can support you gaining more perspective about your element.

Metal   Water   Wood   Fire   Earth   Air   Ether or InnerG

Draw your Element in the form that it appears!
(ex: Water in the form of rain, an ocean, waterfall, river, ice, or cool mist)

BE with your Element!

Complete this part of your Season of Self-Love **with** your Element! Take some time to be in Nature with your element. It can be a brief walk to a place you visit often, or maybe you'd like to plan a trip to a place you've always desired to see. Be silent. Observe and appreciate this aspect of Nature, which is also a part of you.

How does being there make you feel?

_____
_____
_____
_____

Take a nature bath with all your senses. What do you hear, see, smell, taste, and feel?

_____
_____
_____
_____

Be deeply present there. If you feel moved to, you can leave an offering of gratitude there, in exchange for gathering a small memento to keep with you to remind you of your time.

I RESPECT MYSELF

LET'S CONSIDER SELF RESPECT AS A MEANS OF NOURISHING AND PROTECTING YOUR SELF-LOVE.

I RESPECT MYSELF

What's your personal "Golden Rule"?
_____
_____
_____
_____

What ways do you treat others, that you truly value being treated reciprocally?
_____
_____
_____
_____

Many of us learned our values around respect from our Family environment. Are there any family or community sayings you heard growing up? Write them below:
_____
_____
_____
_____

Reflect on one person you truly respect in your family and why? (ancestral or chosen) Write out or record your thoughts below:

_____
_____
_____
_____

Our Home and Fam impact us profoundly. Here we define FAM as Fundamental common values, resources, and relationships. This can be ancestral or Chosen Relationships. We often hold FAM very close and interact with FAM most frequently, (Physically or Mentally/Emotionally) second to ourselves. These connections can impact how we practice our self-love and self-care. What qualifies people, places, (Plants & Animals) as FAM to you?

_____
_____
_____
_____

How do your Self-Love practices and values overflow into each area of Home and FAM?

_____
_____
_____
_____

List 3 to 5 responses for each area of home *If living alone or preparing to move, explore these ideas and areas around the concept of "home", you envision for your future.

Shared Values

Collective Work and Responsibility, Maintenance of Communal Spaces & Tasks.

Common Interests, Shared Play! Shared Fun, Pleasure, Healthy Social Bonds and Connectivity.

Harmoniously Shared Vision & Intention, Harmonious Personal Life Cycle(s), (Age(s) and Stage(s) of Development (Spiritual, Physical, Mental, Emotional)

Shared Resources: Food, Clothes, Shelter, Security, Wealth Creation

Shared concepts of FAM, Culture, Ancestry

Shared Values: What are your collective shared Values?

_____
_____
_____
_____
_____

Harmoniously Shared Vision and Intention: Is there a shared vision with awareness and consideration of each Individuals Life Cycle/Age, Physical, Mental, Emotional Awareness, Gifts, Needs & Capacity? How do you honor it?

_____
_____
_____
_____
_____

Shared Resources: Home is a shared resource. What are the consensual best practices around food consumption and sharing, clothing/non clothing expression & norms, short/long term guest policy, shelter/utility usage, quiet/mindful hours, Security, wealth creation, collective prosperity?

_____
_____
_____
_____

Shared Concept & Practices of Family, Culture, and Ancestry: (This may include early childhood or adolescent patterning, expectations, spiritual or religious values/taboos, epigenetic Traumas & Treasures). Write them below:

_____
_____
_____
_____

Shared Play, Fun, & Recreation: Including and not limited to Common interests, pleasure, creating and maintaining healthy social bonds and connections. Write them below:

_____
_____
_____
_____

Collective Work and Responsibility: Maintenance of Communal Spaces and Tasks, systems of communication, care, and accountability for the greater wellbeing of all. Write them below:

_____
_____
_____
_____

Does your home reflect the Change and Transformation you are preparing for?
_____
_____
_____
_____
_____

What can you do to reflect your desired change in your home?
_____
_____
_____
_____
_____

Are the people in your home reflections of the shift you desire to make?
_____
_____
_____
_____
_____

How can your home inspire more self-love?

_____
_____
_____
_____

If you do not already have an intentional sacred space in your home designated for empowerment that energizes you, create one.

What does or could it look and feel like?

_____
_____
_____
_____

It may also be beneficial to find a place outside your home, whether in your yard or a park that contributes to your peace, clarity, and InnerG.

Self-Transformation "The ME"

Just as the seed has everything it needs for life, you too have everything you need on the inside.

On the next page is the "Seed of Transformation". Before we Change anything, let's spend time with & highlight what is already within you. Be radically honest with your responses in the pages that follow!

Self-Lover's Only Guidebook

It all starts with a "Seed"

Take a moment to study and draw this pattern called the "Seed of Life". This pattern is found in many things, including cell division and the formation of the human embryo. One meaning is that all life and energy come from the same source and that everything is interconnected.

Seed of Transformation

Inner Transformation creates Outer Change

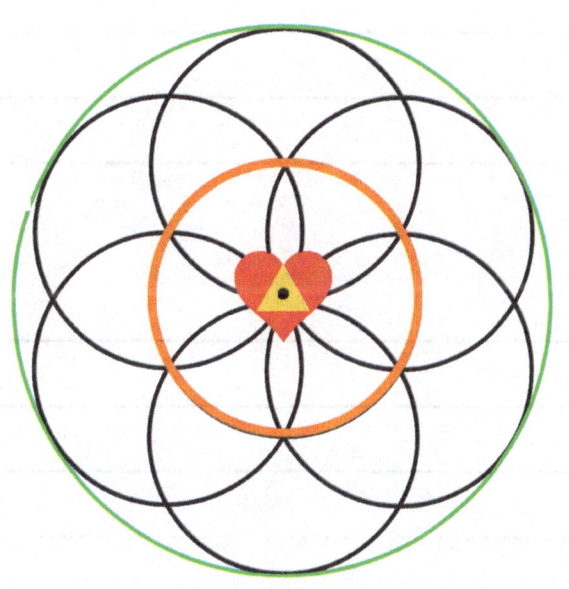

Personal Values

Growth Edges & Opportunities

Gifts & Talents

Hobbies, Interests, & Pleasures

Skills & Experience

Shared Concepts of FAM, Ancestry, & Culture

On the next 2 pages identify and describe 3 to 5 things in each area of your life.

Personal Values:

_____
_____
_____
_____
_____

Gifts & Talents:

_____
_____
_____
_____
_____

Skills & Experience:

_____
_____
_____
_____
_____
_____

FAM, Ancestral & Cultural Values:
_____
_____
_____
_____
_____

Hobbies, Interests, & Pleasures:
_____
_____
_____
_____
_____

Growth Edges and Growth Opportunities:
_____
_____
_____
_____
_____

Draw and label a Seed of Transformation Below

Did you know drawing this pattern of 7 interconnected circles is said to be healing and integrates both hemispheres of the brain!

ANCESTORS

AnceStars

WE ARE MADE OF CLAY AND STARDUST! WE COME FROM OUR PARENTS, THEIR PARENTS ...MULTIPLIED INFINITELY!

Who are your People?
_____
_____
_____
_____

Where were they born and where did they live?
_____
_____
_____
_____

What patterns, preferences, and habits did you learn from them?
_____
_____
_____
_____

Epigenetic memory affects what is passed down and how it expresses in our DNA.

Are these patterns and memories still helpful and relevant for your current goals, D.R.E.A.M. and worldview?

_____
_____
_____
_____
_____

 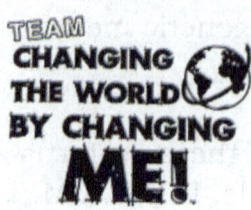

How many generations can you label in your Family Tree?

_____
_____
_____
_____

Place living relatives in the branches above and transitioned relatives below in the roots. Each of us have 4 sets of Ancestors in each generation. Are there any personal or collective stories that inspire you?

_____
_____
_____
_____

Are there any stories or patterns that motivate you to create different choices?

_____
_____
_____
_____

*If Ancestors and/or Elders are unknown, begin your search as able. You may also use your imagination and intuition to describe their qualities and characteristics. Many of our traits are inherited across generations.

Write about your Ancestors (known or intuited) here & in your journal.

*This may be a challenging exercise for many of us. Use your tools, clear your energy, and discuss with a friend, professional, or someone on your personal support T.E.A.M. as needed.

Are there any Collective Ancestors, Historical figures that inspire you?
_____
_____
_____
_____

Who are they and why?
_____
_____
_____
_____

This concludes the end of the ME Phase! You made it! Please review your personal affirmations and any reflections in your journal.

T.E.A.M. WORK

MAKES
THE D.R.E.A.M. WORK

T.E.A.M. Personal Support and Accountability Council

Top 5 + 2

Self

Elder/Expert

Peer

FAM

Friends

Ancestor

Successor

Your Transformation Cycle is a Chrysalis.
You are always at the center of your own T.E.A.M.
Your top 5 + 2 are reflections of where you are going and who you are becoming.
These reflections are Trusted, Supportive, and Vetted.
What qualities within you are amplifying at this time?

You may be a part of many Teams in life, serving in different roles and operating at different levels of commitment. As you Change, Transform, and Achieve your D.R.E.A.M. reality, you are always at the center of your own T.E.A.M. Observe and check in with different trustworthy people in your life regarding your Self Love journey.

Who is on your T.E.A.M.?
_____
_____
_____

Are you reciprocally on their T.E.A.M.?
_____
_____
_____

How do they support your life and accountability to more Self-Love?
_____
_____
_____

Do their Self-Love Values & habits align with your current or future frequency of Self-Love & Care?
_____
_____
_____

*Developing a T.E.A.M. is the focus of the next Season of Change Workbook, in greater detail.

You Made it! You've Arrived! You're Here! Congratulations to YOU and all those that supported your Transformation and Change on your Self-Lover's Journey! Take some time to Celebrate Yourself! What can you do to let all the cells in your being, everyone in your World, on your T.E.A.M. and the Planet know, you are not the same as they knew you before? This can be as simple or as grand as you desire. No steps back! Change is still Changing, and a new season and cycle is underway! Cheers to enjoying life at a whole new octave!

Welcome to the T.E.A.M! Feel Free to share any revelations or feedback with us about your journey at Team@TeamCWCM.com. You may be inspired to attend one of us in person or virtual season group gatherings. Scan the code above to stay in the know.

Self-Lover's Only Guidebook

Self-Love Agreement
"I'm Changing My World, by Changing Me"

Today's date: (How is the weather? What does the moon look like?)

Write the Name You choose and agree to FULLY Respond to within yourself while contributing your best effort to the process:

_____

(This could be your given name, or a chosen name that represents the Change you are committed to making in your life)

I, (Name above) AM_____ **by**_____
                         I'm Changing My World, by Changing Me

(What are you committed to do?)   (How are you committed to doing this?)

FOR Your SELF-LOVERS' Journey, AN EXAMPLE CAN BE, "I _____ AM COMMITTED TO LOVING MYSELF MORE BY_____

This is an agreement with yourself to center self-love and give your best effort to the process for 90+1 days, or however long it takes. The results and rate of transformation reflects your effort. Know that you are supported and connected to real people, navigating real changes Worldwide, living and thriving in their Inner Transformation & desired Change! Notice any resistance. Speak KINDLY to yourself, silence the inner critic and encourage yourself to stay open.

We invite you to set aside at least an hour alone in a peaceful environment. Be as intentional as possible curating the time and space where you will start your journey. Create a space that stimulates all your senses (Smell, taste, touch, sights, and sound.) This could include your favorite food, encouraging playlist or song, favorite outfit, or something good against your skin, incense, oil, or candle. Choose an item that represents Self-love and your desired Change to you. You will keep this in a place you can see or carry it with you over the next few weeks and months. Who you desire to be is already deep within you. Thank you for taking this opportunity, transforming and bringing more of the renewed you out. This time is the "1" in your 90+1 day journey.

During this time write and draw the changes you see taking place in your life in the upcoming Season of Self-Love. Be as specific as possible, add colors, textures, go all in! (and out!) This is your time, your celebration and visioning of how you desire to transform and thrive in your own life! By the end of this section of this Guide, or possibly by the end of the book, your intended focus may slightly or completely Change! That's ok.

Change starts from within and radiates outward. There's nothing outside of you that isn't YOU!

By NOW this is easy review for you. Repetition doesn't hurt! As you Transform within, your perception Changes, your consciousness expands, Your awareness Changes. The World around you Changes. Change is constant. We hope you have grown deeper in your self-love and acceptance, can recognize the seasons and cycles of Change in your life, and are able to adapt with greater ease.

External Changes can be gratifying, like cleaning a room, changing your hair style, or a change in scenery. Changes from within, or internal Transformation may take more time however the effects last much longer. What does the voice of Change inside your head sound like? Is it a kind voice? Is it a Non-Judging Voice? Encouraging voice? Is it a comparing or competitive voice that does not consider the ideas, feelings and needs of others? Have you listened to your Self Love voice memo recordings today?

Where are you with Change now?

On the following page is a general reference of how the TeamCWCM Seasons & Cycles of Change operate. Virtual and limited in person events within the TeamCWCM network happen each Season and Change Cycle.

Just as there are times and conditions most ideal to plant seeds, or to harvest crops, to plan & take a trip, or start a project; there are ideal times to focus on creating Self-Transformation & External Change in our lives. Change is happening within and around us all the time. Aligning our inner efforts with the natural rhythms, seasons, and cycles of nature can benefit our efforts tremendously.

Change & Transformation begin in the Mind. Any time is the right time to start!

Contact an authorized TeamCWCM Transformation Facilitator for custom and specific support for you or your T.E.A.M. at teamcwcm@gmail.com or visit www.teamcwcm.com.

TeamCWCM Seasons of Change
& Cycle of Transformation

Four Seasons of Change

Internal Transformation

WE (WORLD)
Harvest Season,
Connect & Communicate
Celebrate with
All Community Networks,
Evaluate Wins, Vision Forward

ME (SELF)
Inner Work,
Shadow Season,
Internal Alchemy,
Rest, Stillness,
Value Assesment

TEAM
Fortify your TEAM &
Accountability Council
Refine & Further Goals,
Circulate Resources amongst
Mutual Support Networks

DREAM
Renewed Vision
New Growth
Activate New Intentions
Expand Goals, Update Agreements
Implement New Strategies

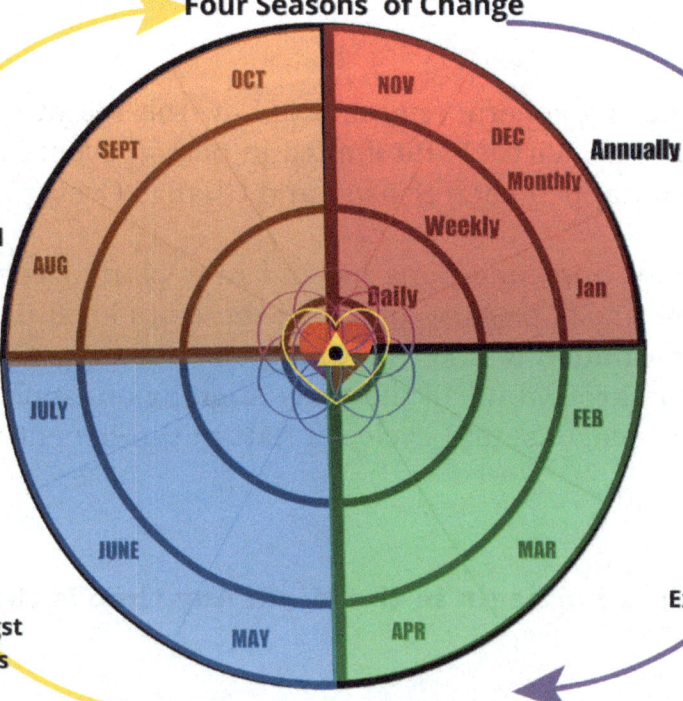

One Continuous & Evolving Cycle

What's Your Purpose?

What are you committed to Changing in your World within?

What are you committed to Changing in the World around you?

What's Your D.R.E.A.M.?

Who's on Your T.E.A.M.?

What are Your Consistent Practices & Routines?

I'm Changing MY World by Changing ME

Self-Lover's Only Guidebook

What's Your Purpose?
_____
_____

What are you committed to Changing in your World within?
_____
_____

What are you committed to Changing in the World around you?
_____
_____

What's Your D.R.E.A.M.?
_____
_____

Who's on Your T.E.A.M.?
_____
_____

What are Your Consistent Practices & Routines?
_____
_____

I'm Changing MY World by Changing ME

TeamCWCM invites YOU to a 90 + 1 day journey of …Self-Initiated, Self-Motivated, Guided Support towards YOUR Self Designed Thriving Change & Transformation

1 HOUR

• Self-Love, Self-Care, Self-Esteem Building Daily Rituals, Routines, & practices optimizing physical, mental-emotional wellness.

1 HOUR

• Self-Observation, Self-Inquiry, Self-Exploration, Meditation, Journaling, Mindful, non-judgmental, Reflection.

1 HOUR

• Self-Cultivation, Building & Refining Skills, opportunities & support networks centering the expression of your talents & gifts.

1 HOUR

• Service & Equitable Value Exchange serving those you are in direct community with, through your skills, gifts, incarnate purpose, aligned with your D.R.E.A.M. Lifestyle Vision, allowing equitable reciprocity.

TeamCWCM is a worldwide network of people, places, events, resources, practices and innovative ideas that inspire a culture and lifestyle of individual self-transformation, while fostering healthy, sustainable collective social change in harmony with Nature and the planet

Our mission ("the work") is to offer relevant and engaging inspirational, developmentally adaptable events and programming that:

- Create authentic connection and healthy space to share victories, challenges, resources, and perspectives centering our shared base common denominators as human beings sharing the planet.

- Create healthy consensual opportunities to know people of differing cultures and communities directly and authentically, deprograming false perspectives often perpetuated without direct healthy experiences.

- Expand conscious awareness of self, centering self-love, in healthy relationship to all sentient beings and the planet.

- Deepen relationship with self, others, and the planet, creating awareness and pathways to personal and collective liberation utilizing social & natural rhythms, seasons, & cycles in correlation to nature & the planet.

- Offer programs and self-transformative tools such as Meditation, Tai 'Chi, Yoga, Reiki and other natural modalities of wellness, healing, empowerment and expression.

- Empower place-based identity, celebrating culture, nature, and highlighting unique similarities and differences amongst places and people.

- Become better stewards of the planet!

TeamCWCM is a Methodology & Network of GlocalSoul Edutainment
TeamCWCM Fundamental concepts, terms and definitions:
This Glossary is a living breathing body of knowledge...

Concepts are drawn from Nature, physics, the Cosmos, timeless global indigenous traditions, and currently trending human consciousness. These concepts, terms and definitions will shift over time based upon Changes on the planet, and the interaction of the TeamCWCM gnosis with individuals, groups, and organizations globally. Our intention is to share a fundamental and complete understanding of the terms shared in our Methodology, in order to empower the base shared common denominator of conscious human awareness. It is our hope that this guide will be translated into multiple languages and code, moving into the future....
*Concepts are not in alphabetical order. They are listed in relevance to comprehending this guide.

SELF (ME) is the primary relationship experience with existence, we are naturally sovereign, autonomous, and interdependent beings. All relationships and connections are reflections and extensions of our relationship with self. This is the cornerstone of this Guide! Corresponding Affirmation: **"I love Myself"**

FAM- is the fundamental primary relationship(s) and access to people and foundational resources essential to individual & collective healthy development... FAM can be comprised of direct familial ancestry, chosen kindred, and extended primary relationships. These relationships influence & form primary patterns in development. Ideally, these relationships can empower us to be centered in our authentic being. It's important to evaluate the health of FAM-ilial relationships during our Changes and cycles of life. These bonds, or lack of, tend to be the most consistent interactions over the course of one's life.
*FAM also includes domestic Partnerships & Relationships-detailed in further studies (TeamCWCM TCG: Octave 2)

FAM may or may not share the physical structure of "home" which includes concepts of:
-Shared Values & Philosophy
-Shared Intentions & aligned cycles of growth
-Food, shelter, clothes, wealth creation
-Shared Work/Maintenance/home upkeep (adornments & hygiene)
-Shared interests and collective play
-Shared Ancestry, Cultural View, which may include Shared subconscious Traumas/Complimentary Healing attractions
Corresponding Affirmation: **"I Respect Myself"**

Self-Lover's Only Guidebook

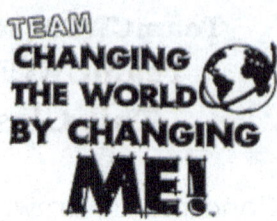

Self-Love is the foundation on your journey of Change and Transformation

	S	M	T	W	T	F	S
Self-Love, Self-Care, Esteem Building Routine							
Self-Inquiry, Observation, Mindful Reflection							
Skill and Talent Cultivation & Refinement							
Sharing Gifts, Talents, Skill in your networks reciprocally							
*							
*							

*These categories are TeamCWCM Suggested areas of focus to optimize Sustainable Change and Self Transformation towards your desired results.

Feel free to add specific activities or practices that best serve you.

Week 1

Self-Lover's Only Guidebook

	S	M	T	W	T	F	S

How did you honor each part of you today?

_____

_____

How much quality time and presence did you share with you? (Your body, your goals, D.R.E.A.M.s, Vision?

_____

_____

What did you do? Where did you go? Most of all, how did you feel?

_____

_____

Do you feel complete? Are you Satiated?

_____

_____

*Ideally this is time centering yourself. If you have those in your life you can share presence with and be completely alone, then possibly consider sharing space. If alone time is not so abundant, communicate you are in an intentional practice of self-love for this season.

Week 2

Self-Lover's Only Guidebook

	S	M	T	W	T	F	S

How did you honor each part of you today?

_____

_____

How much quality time and presence did you share with you? (Your body, your goals, D.R.E.A.M.s, Vision?

_____

_____

What did you do? Where did you go? Most of all, how did you feel?

_____

_____

Do you feel complete? Are you Satiated?

_____

_____

*Ideally this is time centering yourself. If you have those in your life you can share presence with and be completely alone, then possibly consider sharing space. If alone time is not so abundant, communicate you are in an intentional practice of self-love for this season.

Week 3

Self-Lover's Only Guidebook

	S	M	T	W	T	F	S

How did you honor each part of you today?

_____

_____

How much quality time and presence did you share with you? (Your body, your goals, D.R.E.A.M.s, Vision?

_____

_____

What did you do? Where did you go? Most of all, how did you feel?

_____

_____

Do you feel complete? Are you Satiated?

_____

_____

*Ideally this is time centering yourself. If you have those in your life you can share presence with and be completely alone, then possibly consider sharing space. If alone time is not so abundant, communicate you are in an intentional practice of self-love for this season.

Week 4

Self-Lover's Only Guidebook

	S	M	T	W	T	F	S

How did you honor each part of you today?

_____

_____

How much quality time and presence did you share with you? (Your body, your goals, D.R.E.A.M.s, Vision?

_____

_____

What did you do? Where did you go? Most of all, how did you feel?

_____

_____

Do you feel complete? Are you Satiated?

_____

_____

*Ideally this is time centering yourself. If you have those in your life you can share presence with and be completely alone, then possibly consider sharing space. If alone time is not so abundant, communicate you are in an intentional practice of self-love for this season.

Week 5

Self-Lover's Only Guidebook

	S	M	T	W	T	F	S

How did you honor each part of you today?

_____

_____

How much quality time and presence did you share with you? (Your body, your goals, D.R.E.A.M.s, Vision?

_____

_____

What did you do? Where did you go? Most of all, how did you feel?

_____

_____

Do you feel complete? Are you Satiated?

_____

_____

*Ideally this is time centering yourself. If you have those in your life you can share presence with and be completely alone, then possibly consider sharing space. If alone time is not so abundant, communicate you are in an intentional practice of self-love for this season.

Week 6

Self-Lover's Only Guidebook

	S	M	T	W	T	F	S

How did you honor each part of you today?

_____

_____

How much quality time and presence did you share with you? (Your body, your goals, D.R.E.A.M.s, Vision?

_____

_____

What did you do? Where did you go? Most of all, how did you feel?

_____

_____

Do you feel complete? Are you Satiated?

_____

_____

*Ideally this is time centering yourself. If you have those in your life you can share presence with and be completely alone, then possibly consider sharing space. If alone time is not so abundant, communicate you are in an intentional practice of self-love for this season.

Week 7

Self-Lover's Only Guidebook

	S	M	T	W	T	F	S

How did you honor each part of you today?

_____

_____

How much quality time and presence did you share with you? (Your body, your goals, D.R.E.A.M.s, Vision?

_____

_____

What did you do? Where did you go? Most of all, how did you feel?

_____

_____

Do you feel complete? Are you Satiated?

_____

_____

*Ideally this is time centering yourself. If you have those in your life you can share presence with and be completely alone, then possibly consider sharing space. If alone time is not so abundant, communicate you are in an intentional practice of self-love for this season.

Week 8  Self-Lover's Only Guidebook

	S	M	T	W	T	F	S

How did you honor each part of you today?

_____

_____

How much quality time and presence did you share with you? (Your body, your goals, D.R.E.A.M.s, Vision?

_____

_____

What did you do? Where did you go? Most of all, how did you feel?

_____

_____

Do you feel complete? Are you Satiated?

_____

_____

*Ideally this is time centering yourself. If you have those in your life you can share presence with and be completely alone, then possibly consider sharing space. If alone time is not so abundant, communicate you are in an intentional practice of self-love for this season.

Week 9  Self-Lover's Only Guidebook

	S	M	T	W	T	F	S

How did you honor each part of you today?

_____

_____

How much quality time and presence did you share with you? (Your body, your goals, D.R.E.A.M.s, Vision?

_____

_____

What did you do? Where did you go? Most of all, how did you feel?

_____

_____

Do you feel complete? Are you Satiated?

_____

_____

*Ideally this is time centering yourself. If you have those in your life you can share presence with and be completely alone, then possibly consider sharing space. If alone time is not so abundant, communicate you are in an intentional practice of self-love for this season.

Week 10  Self-Lover's Only Guidebook

	S	M	T	W	T	F	S

How did you honor each part of you today?

_____

_____

How much quality time and presence did you share with you? (Your body, your goals, D.R.E.A.M.s, Vision?

_____

_____

What did you do? Where did you go? Most of all, how did you feel?

_____

_____

Do you feel complete? Are you Satiated?

_____

_____

*Ideally this is time centering yourself. If you have those in your life you can share presence with and be completely alone, then possibly consider sharing space. If alone time is not so abundant, communicate you are in an intentional practice of self-love for this season.

Week 11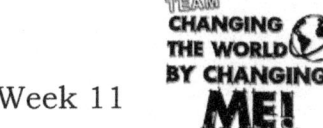

	S	M	T	W	T	F	S

How did you honor each part of you today?

_____

_____

How much quality time and presence did you share with you? (Your body, your goals, D.R.E.A.M.s, Vision?

_____

_____

What did you do? Where did you go? Most of all, how did you feel?

_____

_____

Do you feel complete? Are you Satiated?

_____

_____

*Ideally this is time centering yourself. If you have those in your life you can share presence with and be completely alone, then possibly consider sharing space. If alone time is not so abundant, communicate you are in an intentional practice of self-love for this season.

Week 12  Self-Lover's Only Guidebook

	S	M	T	W	T	F	S

How did you honor each part of you today?

_____

_____

How much quality time and presence did you share with you? (Your body, your goals, D.R.E.A.M.s, Vision?

_____

_____

What did you do? Where did you go? Most of all, how did you feel?

_____

_____

Do you feel complete? Are you Satiated?

_____

_____

*Ideally this is time centering yourself. If you have those in your life you can share presence with and be completely alone, then possibly consider sharing space. If alone time is not so abundant, communicate you are in an intentional practice of self-love for this season.

Week 13  Self-Lover's Only Guidebook

	S	M	T	W	T	F	S

How did you honor each part of you today?

_____

_____

How much quality time and presence did you share with you? (Your body, your goals, D.R.E.A.M.s, Vision?

_____

_____

What did you do? Where did you go? Most of all, how did you feel?

_____

_____

Do you feel complete? Are you Satiated?

_____

_____

*Ideally this is time centering yourself. If you have those in your life you can share presence with and be completely alone, then possibly consider sharing space. If alone time is not so abundant, communicate you are in an intentional practice of self-love for this season.

LIFE WORK

The following pages can be printed

Self-Lover's Only Guidebook

7. I AM Changing My World By Changing Me
6. I AM A MasterPeace
5. I AM Because We Are
4. I Value My Unique Individuality
3. I Believe In Myself
2. I Respect Myself
1. I Love Myself

AFFIRMATIONS OF CHANGE

Self-Lover's Only Guidebook

89

Self-Lover's Only Guidebook

	S	M	T	W	T	F	S

How did you honor each part of you today?

_____

_____

How much quality time and presence did you share with you? (Your body, your goals, D.R.E.A.M.s, Vision?

_____

_____

What did you do? Where did you go? Most of all, how did you feel?

_____

_____

Do you feel complete? Are you Satiated?

_____

_____

*Ideally this is time centering yourself. If you have those in your life you can share presence with and be completely alone, then possibly consider sharing space. If alone time is not so abundant, communicate you are in an intentional practice of self-love for this season.

Self-Lover's Only Guidebook

Self-Love Agreement
"I'm Changing My World, by Changing Me"

(How is the weather? What does the moon look like?)

Write the Name You choose and agree to FULLY Respond to within yourself while contributing your best effort to the process:

_____

(This could be your given name, or a chosen name that represents the Change you are committed to making in your life)

I, (Name above) AM_____by_____
I'm Changing My World, by Changing Me

(What are you committed to do?)   (How are you committed to doing this?)

FOR Your SELF-LOVERS' Journey, AN EXAMPLE CAN BE, "I _____ AM COMMITTED TO LOVING MYSELF MORE BY_____

This is an agreement with yourself to center self-love and give your best effort to the process for 90+1 days, or however long it takes. The results and rate of transformation reflects your effort. Know that you are supported and connected to real people, navigating real changes Worldwide, living and thriving in their Inner Transformation & desired Change! Notice any resistance. Speak kindly to yourself, silence the inner critic, and encourage yourself to stay open.

We invite you to set aside an hour alone in a peaceful environment. Be as intentional as possible curating the time and space where you will start your journey. Create a space that stimulates all your senses (Smell, taste, touch, sights, and sound.)
This could include your favorite food, encouraging playlist or song, favorite outfit, or something good against your skin, incense, oil, or candle. Choose an item that represents Self-love and your desired Change to you. You will keep this in a place you can see or carry it with you over the next few weeks and months. Who you desire to be is already deep within you. Thank you for taking this opportunity, transforming, and bringing more of the renewed you out. This day serves as the "1" in your 90+1 day journey.

During this time write and draw the changes you see taking place in your life in the upcoming Season of Self-Love. Be as specific as possible, add colors, textures, go all in! (and out!) This is your time, your celebration and visioning of how you desire to transform and thrive in your own life! By the end of this section of this Guide, or possibly by the end of the book, your intended focus may slightly or completely Change! That's ok.

TeamCWCM is a program and platform of GlocalSoul Edutainment. Inspire, Entertain, Educate, Empower! Learn more, support, book a workshop, donate at www.glocalsouledu.com

Made in the USA
Coppell, TX
11 February 2026

71764724R00057